good
beast

good
beast

Andrew Michael Roberts

Burnside Review Press   Portland, Oregon

good beast
© 2015 Andrew Michael Roberts

Cover Image: *Falling Mid-silent*
by May Chua, whitehorsegrey

Cover Design: Regina Godfrey
Layout: Shira Richman

Printed in the U.S.A.
First Edition, 2015
ISBN: 978-0-9895611-5-0

Burnside Review Press
Portland, Oregon
www.burnsidereview.org

Burnside Review Press titles are available for purchase from the
publisher and Small Press Distribution (www.spdbooks.org).

This book is for Tim.

death star   **: a history in fragments**

death star	15
the dreamless and the meek	16
god bless the guns and the gorgeous morning stars	18
little bastards	19
november and its sunken sky and the swallowing of beasts	20
rebel spy	21
intelligence	22
fingers	23
give your grandmother a kiss	24
dreamers and heathens	25
the storm troopers	26
escape pod	27
what fear is	28
easter 1982	29
meat and bones	30
while the barn swallows slice and arc	32
the force	33
while we sleep under the covers with our flashlights lit	34
a beast in the river	35
closing credits	36

good beast

anthem	41
the golden arm	48
holy rollers	54
good beast	56
flipbook of the dead	58

thunder & gristle

that poet, the sea   65
don't believe in yourself   66
killing me softly   68
poem at night   70
we bruise, we are draped in a fine-haired skin   72
a day arrives without its color   74
darkling prophet   75
the stars are famished   76
thunder & gristle   79

absences

when i die and return to the world as a stone   85
the sea in our bones   87
for an uncle dying in august   89
geometry of innocence   90
graves   92
song for the day after independence day   93
when we all up and vanish at last   94

death
star

: a
history
in
fragments

death
star

perhaps
someplace
beyond thought

and prayer

and all
possibility

a tiny
nucleus of pain
exists,

and the
galaxies

are pinned to it,

and frayed
out,

like a flag.—

that's our
flag.

••••

the
dreamless
and
the
meek

darth vader
and the devil
take turns
looking
after us

while the angels
take their
pall mall breaks.

vader pays
a quarter
if you rub
his back

and shut
your whiny
mouth.

lucifer
in his crown
of skulls

looking
over
the lawn

scattered with
hens and
concrete elk

convinces us
there is
no god.

i blame him
for this
lonely
feeling

when i pray.

••••

god
bless
the
guns
and
the
gorgeous
morning
stars

to crawl
across the
woodshed roof,

concealed
inside a sea
of firs,—

scent of
chickenshit
and civet cats—

to look
down upon

those unloved
neighbor boys,

who take
a blowtorch to

a dead
eagle they

dragged home.

••••

little
bastards

your step-
father's

nicaraguan
machete,

his air rifle too,

while he
sleeps off

graveyard
shift.

look how we
annihilate

his
foam wolverine.

••••

november
and
its
sunken
sky
and
the
swallowing
of
beasts

hello,
stranglehold
of rain.

overnight
your creeks
rose up

and took
the forest
by its teeth.

downstream's
a horse strung
in a fence.

he isn't ours.

the river came
and went

and kept
his skin.

••••

rebel
spy

machete me
a nest

in the sword ferns

where only the
moss and
millipedes

and starlings
know.—

darth vader
at a distance,

smoking in
the yard
over the
evaporated
pond,

reaching out
to touch his
reflection

with such
tenderness,

it scatters
the chickens.

••••

intelligence

no one
looks up.

you can
perch there

on a lichen-
bearded limb

like an
absence

among
shadows

and find out
everything.

••••

fingers

the devil
with his hand
in my lap,

whispering
the name

of that lonely
pedophile
up the road

asleep
in his
red trailer

ringed with
starved hounds.

engine parts.

gunshot
gallon cans.

••••

give
your
grandmother
a
kiss

i recall
the cannula's
forked throat,

the caramel scent
of oxygen in it.

her soft and
wasted cheek.

nicotine.

lipstick on
the filter of

a just-sucked
cigarette.

••••

**dreamers
and
heathens**

we made a
snow-
man

in the
sideyard,

and then
crucified
him,

and
gave him
tits.

••••

25

**the
storm
troopers**

above us
while we
pray

our drunken
angels

crush their
beer cans

on the
trailer roof:

o the frozen
drifting
howls!

their ashtrays

of
punched
snow.

••••

escape
pod

darth vader
doesn't believe
in snow.

he cleans
his guns

in the tv room.

at the quarry
we close
each other

inside
a dead
refrigerator

and bobsled it
across

the reservoir
ice.

••••

**what
fear
is**

dear
beelzebub,

there's a secret
power
in it:

i once saw
six geese

wild with hate

corner
a steer

and make him
kick a steel

fence
down.

••••

easter
1982

they found that
lost girl

six miles
downriver

wrapped in
tyvek

and barbed
wire.

what was
her name?

who
loved her?

••••

meat
and
bones

when he failed
to call it to the
surface with a
spatula he
tried the
handle of
a rake,

and when
that failed
he used
a garden hose,
and when
the skin
still held

and the in-
visible stars
all at once
screamed out
his name

and firing a
colt anaconda
.44 magnum
into the trees
made no
difference,

he padlocked
the singlewide shut
with everyone

inside and
set it on fire,

and when he
failed even
at that he

laid himself out
on a cot in the
smoke shed

with a lifted
paramedic kit
flung open

and a syringe
choked with
demerol

slipped to his
medial
cubital
vein,

and
that
did it.

••••

while	the girls
the	upstream
barn	will masturbate
swallows	their stallion
slice	if you
and	ask them
arc	right.

• • • •

**the
force**

dear darth
vader,

o to be
tucked
in

each night

by the same
hands

that
struck you

until you
saw stars.

••••

while
we
sleep
under
the
covers
with
our
flashlights
lit

it waits
in each of us,

curled into
its nest
of lungs,

thumping
from a dream

to see
if it's safe

out here
in the light.

••••

**a
beast
in
the
river**

dear lucifer,

the way
you cross
my arms

against my ribs
so tenderly,

and kiss me
on the eyes:

i only
pretend
to sleep.

night is
the island

i've been
swimming
toward.—

••••

**closing
credits**

and in
the darkness i

haul my
carcass up
into the
riverweeds

to lie alone
among
the insect
screams,

the current's
sigh

unfurling
its years,

and uncurl
my star-
speckled arms,

and dissolve
into a rising

snow of moths,

engulfing
the sky,—

and become
everything.

good
beast

anthem

world,

let us take
one another for granted,

while over the t-ball
fields

the evening sun
is a pink disturbance

in the poplar leaves,

and warm upon
the asphalt

a girl who was born
without fibulas

lines her plastic horses up
inside a corral of chalk.

these horses, who
close their eyes,

waiting to be named:
with a magnifying glass

she commands the sun
to be merciless.

••••

when god was
in love,

he looked down upon us
so long

he left a cast of his face
on the film of the sky.

now it fills with
meteorites.

it grows a mane
of dark smoke,

smoke that a line
of cranes

runs through like a
finger.

—these nonchalant cranes,
touching

the xerox of god.

••••

tonight the reservoir
is full

of itself,
a body so black

it believes it is
weightless

and infinite
and pricked

with innumerable
diamonds

of long-suffering light.

••••

and it occurs to me,
i am not unlike

a prosthetic leg
you remove in the evening

with great relief
and lean against an armoire

while you massage
the nerve endings

back to life.

••••

one day in 1983
i was the best

math student in all
of idaho.

for a prize they gave me
a milk goat to raise

and a robotic chicken
to replicate.

at the apex of my
genius,

i had a whole farm
of unfeeling beasts.

••••

i was a child,

i was one hundred
thousand years old:

through a cloud
of dust

the caravan came
and went,

leaving us the girl
with a heart full of bees,

the conjoined jesuses,
and the pony

with a muzzle of gold.

••••

when summer pours
its soul

into the city,

i forget myself
among

the concrete cliffs
and become

an echelon
of honeyed light.

••••

world,
we are

something
of a mirror:

you are one
who claims

to dislike the scent
of gasoline,

while i keep
a collection of birds

who mistook
window glass

for actual air.

••••

while somewhere
in a dream

a vaux swift
makes a penthouse

of your skull,

and too soon
from the woods

barking our old names
come the dogs

we'd forgotten
wearing masks

of the people we loved.

••••

at such times
there are
questions

one should
ask oneself.

••••

world, look
at your
chimneys,

ringed with
wet crows.

**the
golden
arm**

dear x,
when i begin again

to see the arc
of existence

as an asterisk
god painted on
a gypsy moth

for whom reality
is a series

of random decisions
made within

a one mile radius
of the chinese
baptist church

and its perfect
uninhabitable lawns,

i muster and rise
and go down
to the reservoir

at dusk when
the horseshoe pits
have gone still,

and walk
the gravel path

past the story
the pond tells

of recently surrendering

to its own
toxic algae,

and sit along
a concrete lip

to name the
artificial swans
drifting there.

••••

because which of us
has not

at one time
or another

against or
according to
our wish

become a replacement?

••••

regarding your inquiry
about the arm:

here in the park
with only the sprinklers
and snails

i may at last
unlatch it

and lay it gleaming
upon my lap
with some relief

while around me
the day's memories fuse

into the molecules
of the grass:

the frantic mastiff
broken loose

racing picnic
to picnic,

the drunk
on his sheet

under the willows,
singing patriotic tunes.

••••

the truth:
it is weighty

and difficult
to articulate,

like a voice
filled with snow.

••••

i am thinking, x,
of you

as i might
the pope,

who if he could
might walk away
one evening

into the alleyways
of rome

only to sleep
unrecognized

in an ancient
statuary,

to wake hungry
and watch

the new green
atmosphere

fill in all that
black empty space.

••••

dear x,
do you see

this story is no longer
about you.

and conjuring suitable names
for swans takes time.

and i stopped believing in you
moments ago.

and this hypothetical
gilded limb you covet—

perhaps if i sit here
in the open
long enough,

lost inside a choice,

someone necessary
will happen along

and carry
it away.

**holy
rollers**

sometimes alone
on the beach

you discover
a footprint
so large

you can't
crawl back out.

and then god
in his galactic crane

lowers over you
a dome of
bedazzling stars.

god and his hard hat:
he will build you a world.

he'll kill you with beauty
if it's the last thing he does.

a gorgeous blinding
swirl of gulls collects,

collects silently
inside you,

where a secret was
once a lie

you told only
your girlfriend,
and god.

well, are you
a man
or a mite,

or entire wildernesses
of sand?

or the crush
of the surf,

or a cosmology
of long-extinguished suns?

below you,
below the ocean,

there is a rainbow
in hell.

screaming.

screaming
anything it wants.

good
beast

seagulls everywhere,
hungry angels.

sick things,
i love you

slicing, gnashing
at the rain,

the selfless
inexplicable
rain you envy.

you know no fear.
i toss the effervescent

wafer of my rage,
and you devour it,

and explode.
your sacrifice
will not

go undeclared.
i dictate a letter:

dear mother,
the wind,

you fucking
banshee—

the birds are
exploding for me.

please include this
in your prayers,

for forgiveness
and peace,

which race wailing
through the sleet,

waking all
creation up

on their way
to the world's

insatiable ear.

**flipbook
of
the
dead**

when he went blue
they shocked my father's

heart so hard it burst
into a confetti of moths

which later fell as a light snow
over iceland.

iceland, which understands
winter darkness like a wife.

••••

rare, this calm
in which i float
out of my skull

while mother
wrings her hands
in a hospital lounge.

••••

life comes along
like gossip

and
carries
you.

••••

snow sliced through
with phosphorescent light:

we step out into it,
offering up our palms.

it is nothing
more holy than ice
falling unrepeatably.

but we can't help
feeling something's
possible

so long as around us
this story keeps
touching

gracefully
down.

••••

what if the afterlife
is all of our mistakes

waiting up for us
in white frocks

at a picnic
in a clovered field

whose edges are
glowy and blurred,

and all we need do
is sit among them

and that tantalizing
feast,

and touch nothing?

••••

a father at rest
in an electronic bed:

my father, yours,
who once
was frightful,

sipping now
from a shaky cup.

half himself.

a troupe of moths
could carry him.

the nurse is tired.
they've taped felt birds

to the windowpane.

••••

walking at night
with the scattered
snow flung black

against the streetlamp's
blaring eye

and the planet sifting
through the ions,

the dark galactic absences,

can you not hear
below the traffic

and slush and
cold barking dogs

the resolute dead
knocking their song

against the ceiling
of the earth?

if you are honest
with yourself.

tell me which
of us is not flesh.

thunder
&
gristle

**that
poet,
the
sea**

there's a
memory i adore

in which i'm
drowning
as a boy,

cradled
by the
undertow,

lulled in
the soft
crushing
certainty,

at home
at last
in the silt
and the roil,

while above
the heaving
surf

a cloud
i love slowly

swallows
its fist.

don't
believe
in
yourself

i'm talking to you,
molotov cocktail.

rare city of no regret.

drunken children
everywhere,
wind without apology.

saddest possible kittens.

time thrives;
statues hurl their
shadows

across a sunset
shamelessly.

: symphony of gutters
and light.

bird mafias.

nights wide awake,
sink holes swallowing

the dreamless
and the meek.

and now
the scarfaced
moon—

moon of milk
and redemption,

rising as if
to believe in us.

the orphaned wolves in us
quaking for a howl.

killing
me
softly

thought i felt
an angel just now
sipping at my jugular.

o ecstasy of almost!

life, at times, throbs
like a pivotal sonnet
from the collected poems
of captain caveman.

nearly nectar for the gods:
i am outlandishly gorgeous,
yet lacking that certain
je ne sais quoi.

if he were alive in this
terrible time, cervantes
might write a song about me
tinged with blind trust

and call it
on my way to absence.

go away, angels.
i'm having trouble
reconciling god.

i'm mediocre,
pallid, and diffuse.

i keep dreaming
of terrible loneliness.

poem
at
night

but for the tiny
pitiable grievances
of the stars,

i would sleep.
but for the daphne
at the window

sealed up
in the moonlight
saying, finally, —no.

i would sleep
inside my soft
history of skin.

beside you i would sleep
but for your softness
faintly glowing.

—if deepest night
would arrive,
a black snow

to flutter down
and enfold
us.

but for
bright mercury
and pride,

i would
touch you
through the drifts.

we
bruise,
we
are
draped
in
a
fine-
haired
skin

aren't we a noisesome
fragile kind of fruit,

blameless and plumping
in the unencumbered sun.—

while some toxic
seed has cracked, and

now we're pregnant
with a slow and secret poison.

you can see it in the open
palms of our eyes.

we are diminished and full
of new words for it:

apocrypha.
luminescence.

today a flock of
songbirds attacked

the morning traffic.
great silence gave way

to the embrace of glass
and bone. not to worry,

a satellite is circling
over each of us.

you can feel a subtle
hum, a frequency in

the sapwood buzzing
your brief existence.

from your loving ignorant tree,
look up: the contrails,

the wingfeathers,
the improbable blue.

a periodic glint of foil
lodged reassuringly

like a sliver
in the skin of the sky.

a
day
arrives
without
its
color

diego rivera
has finally
finished dreaming.

has left us,
and taken the new
morning with him,

and the neighborhood
birds without blame
or offense,

and strung
their
dark trees

with families
of faceless
unnamed

singing clocks.

**darkling
prophet**

i admire the moon's
ability to give
a shit less.

that cold,
lonely job.

there are no
real angels
on the moon,

only snow angels
a forgotten
astronaut made

looking down upon
the blue world
that birthed him.

now and then
i miss something
terribly.

what is it.

**the
stars
are
famished**

walt whitman,
there has been so
little rain.

and yet
there you go,
wild-bearded,
wet-lipped
into the wilderness,

sniffing the wild-
flower corpses,
strolling the empty
creekbottoms,

touching each
lost fish as if
it would now
rise up and swim!

full of faith and guile.

you speak
to the trees
as if their hearts
were little bright fires
stoked by your
vast loneliness.

no rain, and yet
you stroke
the choked grasses
tender as
a grandfather
abandoned to
the fenced lawns
of a convalescent home.—

and yet there you are,
toiling on a far
bald butte,

recalling the green
rituals of spring,

looking over
the clear-cuts
with kind
otherworldly eyes,

building your great
and terrible ark.

o america. o hatrack
of handsome crowns.

o bottomless love,
nectar of hope

and skeletons
and infinitesimal
miracles.

walter, i believe
in you.

thunder
&
gristle

america
the beautiful, i
hereby believe
in astro-turf
and mother-of-pearl
and the rising
of christ

to god's
golden bosom
like a dearly
beloved bread,

scent of molasses
and angelfire.

••••

belief, i've come
to understand,
is consequential
and sexy.

i believe, for example,
in this obsolete
map of ohio,

this ladybird beetle
flexing one wing
against a window pane
in the lightning-strike light

: lone things nestled
into their beauty
like larvae.

••••

god bless
a lot of things, right?

god bless seven-
eleven and
chick-o-sticks
and methotrexate

and the small
child torturing
a newt
with his father's
bar-b-que wand.

god rest ye
accidentally impaled
javelin coaches.

god bless my love
of pinochle vs.
the gritty tale
of a troupe
of lungworms
navigating a kitty-

litter labyrinth
on their way
to my alveoli.

the lord loves
david bowie
and harvey milk

and the have-nots
amassing on
the outskirts,
blasting their
boomboxes against
a great
gathering deafness.

••••

all you've got to do
is win.

o great travesty
of smurfs!

o u-turn
of gazelles,
school of
shimmering terns.

sunrise over
walla walla washington,

its orange-
skinned snow.

its exhausted
children.

••••

america,
i can't look me
fully in the eye.

but you.
reckless,
unbreakable
you—

touch me
with the wingtip
of your dream,

and all the
mechanical wrens
of possibility

begin to blink.

absences

when
i
die
and
return
to
the
world
as
a
stone

i shall at long last lie still,
and without hope

or despair,
awaiting no one,

go unnoticed in the rain
with my smock of glazed leaves.

and be crowned
by whichever beetle

ascends me.
twigs and their shadows.

king of nothing
i shall not dream,

nor contain galaxies,
nor remember

what missing is,
or that i loved,

but simply exist while a cloud
and its entourage

of crows slip across
the crest of the sky.

in their presence and
their absence i shall begin.

i'll begin
where the silences

forget themselves
between silences.

the
sea
in
our
bones

when the glaciers
in the end

have shed their teeth

and sloughed
into the surf,

and the rains persist,
and the seas crawl forth,

our mouths
become zeroes,

when the froth
and salt

inhabit our lungs,
and bridges wilt,

and sharks patrol
the avenues,

when at the surface
the toy boats drift,

abuzz with flies,

and when the flies
at last have given

up their ghosts,

what then
but stillness?

the echoes of god.

blue and blue
and blue.

the waterbirds
preening as if

the sun will set
and rise again,

and history fail,
and the mountains

be forgotten,

and the swell
of the deep

become what has
always been

and will always be.

for
an
uncle
dying
in
august

when you depart
in the morning
brilliant with longing,

and the slow light
settles into place
between us,

and the clouds
track across
their cellophane rails,

and the moths rise
from their nests
of dew,

and nothing spoken
is more necessary
than silence,

we will be silent then
while you ease
away from yourself

and begin
to break up
into everything,

leaving the atmosphere
of our small
understanding.

geometry
of
innocence

god is dreaming.

a colony of moths
unfurls in the mind,
a fortress

of trees
gowned in smoke
through which you fall
sideways, like a leaf.

at the lakeshore,
walk softly. water sleeps.

light buzzes
in the crustaceans' brains.

in the distance
the mountains
with their eyes of ice
strike out against
the thunder-vaults.

egrets, egrets
if they succeed:
unfolding to take
the place of the sky.

all shall be showered
in otherworldly poise.

here is a throne
while you wait
made of driftwood
and bone.

and your
ignorance crown,

for which
the world wars.

graves

i do not believe
in death.

i come because
the silence
is deepest,

and people abandon
marvelous things:

fossils, teeth,
a barbed-wire horse,

birdcages filled
with tv guides.

hand grenades,
each other.

song
for
the
day
after
independence
day

morning has its hangover.

the sun floods bruised
and slow

along the trashed
riverfront,

the streets tattooed
with gunpowder
burns.

they're out there in it:
the dispirited,

heavy in the legs,
jangling empty
leashes,

filling up
the alleyways

with the names
of the lost.

when
we
all
up
and
vanish
at
last

may our abandoned chickens
inherit the city,

and the hedges rise up,
and the money sigh,

and our scents
lift away from things

slowly like souls,—

souls the seagulls disrupt
in their mad rejoicing

as below them the bears
begin to unearth

all we loved and buried
o those rare and opulent years.

Acknowledgments

Versions of some of these poems were first published by:
Bateau, inter|rupture, jubilat, Parcel, Poetry Society of America, Route 9,
and *Verse.*

The section "death star: a history in fragments" was initially
published as a poem series in *The Seattle Review*.

The phrase "which of us is not flesh" in the poem "flipbook
of the dead" is Kenneth Patchen's. The phrase "geometry
of innocence" is Bob Dylan's. The phrase "the stars are
famished" is James Tate's. The phrase "on my way to absence"
in the poem "killing me softly" is Damien Jurado's. The
phrase "all you've got to do is win" in the poem "thunder &
gristle" is David Bowie's.

Thanks to my wife Sarah, who reads everything first
with graciousness and honesty and love. Thanks to Amy
Dickinson, my dear friend and reader and invaluable
support. To Sara Guest, my friend, reader, advisor, and
listener. To my brother Tim for his inspiration and support.
Thank you to Sid Miller for believing in my poetry. Thanks
to Mom and Dad. Thanks to Murray and Mariette. Thanks
to my friends and colleagues: Mary Ruefle, Carl Adamshick,
Daneen Bergland, Phil Moll, Derrick Travers, Dani
Blackman, Patrick Robbins, Eli Renaud, Tony Wolk, Lindy
Delf, Jake Sepulveda, Tallulah Bleu, Kate Robin, Sarah
Sturdy, and Emily McKissock.

Andrew Michael Roberts is the author of the poetry collection *something has to happen next* from University of Iowa Press, and two chapbooks: *Dear Wild Abandon* from Poetry Society of America and *Give Up* from Tarpaulin Sky Press. He lives with his wife Sarah in Portland, Oregon, where he spends his time as a cardiac nurse, a cyclist, a sasquatch enthusiast, a library regular, and a poet.